by PRIMM

Halloween has come again
And now the Magic will begin
So carve my face a spooky grin
And place a candle there within
Scrape my sides, but not too thin
Wrapped in my orange pumpkin skin

I look out on this haunting night
From where I sit, it all looks right
A night of fun, a night of fright
I lead them all with pumpkin light
On Halloween oh, what a sight
We eat our candy bite by bite

But now the hour's growing late
And all I fear, must face our fate
The Magic soon will dissipate
And my orange skin will desiccate
A memory left to satiate
Our need for Halloween is great

So wrapped in my orange pumpkin skin
I see it all through flames within
And that is why I flash my grin
A part of Halloween I've been
Another year to go, but then
You'll see my glowing pumpkin skin

HALLOWEEN MACHINE AUTUMN 2022   ISBN: 9798355615376   COPYRIGHT 2022 by Paul Counelis

HALLOWEEN MACHINE	**CONTENTS**	AUTUMN 2022
EDITORIAL: HALLOWEEN COMEBACK	Paul Counelis	3
ROB ZOMBIE'S 'THE MUNSTERS'		4
JUST A LITTLE CREEPY	Kurtis Primm	7
USS EDSON: A HAUNTING ON THE RIVER	Paul Counelis	10
HALLOWEEN JOKES	Mark Taylor	13
HALLOWEEN STORE SIGHTINGS		14
60 YEARS OF 'MONSTER MASH'	Paul Counelis	23
THE HANSON HOUSE	Kiddferd P	28
TEN FAMILY FRIGHTFESTS	Paul Counelis	32
THE SNOOPY SHOW: HALLOWEEN		35
MACABRE MUSIC: THE DOORS	Paul Counelis	38
THE HALLOWEEN THAT ALMOST WASN'T		41
OPEN GRAVES	Kurtis Primm	45
THOSE MAGICAL HALLOWEEN NIGHTS!	Paul Counelis	46
HAPPY HALLOWEEN!	Diamond Counelis	47

EDITORIAL: Halloween Magic

By Paul Counelis

WOW! Halloween 2022 is here and it shows that Halloween is back WITH A VENGEANCE! There are SO MANY new things to talk about for this Samhain season, from some amazing new props to a renaissance of fall related cereals and snacks to an ABUNDANCE of treats via the worlds of TV and movies, Halloween 2022 is proving something that many of us already knew…the world needs Halloween!

Of course, that's extra fun news here at the Machine, because it gives us a chance to rundown a bunch of the new stuff and give our take on what the new Halloween commerce has to offer. But it also gives a sense of the marriage between nostalgia and a fresh new Halloween feeling, which is where this holiday excels most; it's what helps to give the magic, year after year.

Because no matter what comes on TV every fall, no matter what cool new costumes and props are on the store shelves, the thing that brings us back to celebrate America's dark holiday year after year is the essence of what makes Halloween so appealing and magical: the imagery. The imagery of yesteryear, the imagery of autumn. The smells and sounds of Halloween night. The days leading up to the final day of October.

At press time there were widely circulated (if unconfirmed) rumors of the "big two" burger companies both bringing in some fun new stuff for Halloween foodies. McDonald's will supposedly have their beloved old trick or treat pails back, and Burger King apparently has a new Halloween Whopper – orange buns and ghost pepper cheese?

Of course, with Halloween goodies, one of the most important (if not THE most important) aspects is the presentation. Do the new cereals give you the good ol' Halloween feeling, for instance? We've corralled them here for your perusal, as well as a nice round-up from SOME of the Halloween displays at the retail stores. As usual, my pals help us with that part.

Speaking of Halloween pals, as usual we have some of our friends here at the Machine helping out with another fun issue. That means our Halloween poet laureate Kurtis Primm is on hand once again, and we would like to dedicate this new issue to Kurtis' mother and father. We celebrate this season in their honor, and to every special loved one who we all remember on our special, hallowed, magical day. Happy Halloween!

A REVIEW BY PAUL COUNELIS

Here is what I love MOST about Rob Zombie...he lives in a world where *Abbott and Costello Meet Dr. Jekyll and Mr. Hyde* gets its own special graphic on the local TV station's creature feature. He has an alternate horror driven universe in his mind and he drops us in it every so often (for better or for worse).

The Munsters is like a bizarre, garish, monster kid fever dream...how the hell is it even a movie? I don't know, but that's what I like about it. It's completely married to its own aesthetic from beginning to end. The colors are like Halloween Skittles splashed all over the entire earth. There are visually arresting long shots followed by the weirdest handheld close-ups, with flashes similar to a much less depraved *House of 1,000 Corpses* (which will always be my fave of his).

4 | HALLOWEEN MACHINE   AUTUMN 2022

As an orthodox narrative, no. This movie does not work. I don't think a bunch of kids are going to clamor for The Munsters based on this flick. It's unsettlingly odd and a lot of the jokes are childish, but not in the way they needed to be for *The Munsters* to have mainstream success. It's wayyy too long to support the flimsy story. It has no real rhythm.

But playing as a midnight movie on a local station's creature feature in the same world as *House of 1,000 Corpses* and RZ's *Halloween*? It not only works but it's kinda awesome. And I won't lie, I love it. It's a world I will revisit because I not only like that aesthetic...I sometimes crave it. I'm drawn to it. It's what I hope for in every RZ movie and I haven't really gotten it since *The Lords of Salem*, and I really didn't expect to find it in the cartoon-y Munsters redux.

In THAT world, the characters of this Munsters movie are complete icons, celebrated and thought of affectionately. The door to that world is open in RZ's mind, the place where old monster movies play all the time, full color posters of 50s monster flicks adorn walls everywhere, and on Halloween night every street is full of the most perfectly imperfectly placed Halloween decor, visually striking and tugging on the magical nostalgia like an old friend.

It's a world where every store uses a black and orange motif with Hammer horror font on all their signs, and the local school spirit week includes a "monster day". Kids rock KISS shirts to the Halloween dance, and Ten Years After's "I'd Love to Change the World" builds to a crescendo somewhere in the airwaves of the crisp autumn night.

When the Abbott and Costello image splashed across my screen early on in the movie, I found that feeling that I most love about RZ's art, and I just settled in for the visuals (and turned off any hope of a "real" movie in the modern sense).

As for the more orthodox take, and I won't pile on knowing that the internet will crap all over the film's many flaws...I thoroughly enjoyed all of these actors, and found it amusing that Richard Brake is now in a PG movie playing a hammy mad scientist type. Roebuck is 100% on point and seems completely at home in his part as Grandpa. Jeff Daniel Phillips plays Herman in a childlike way that (wisely) isn't just another impression of Fred Gwynne. And I'm just gonna say it...I know a bunch of people will cringe...but I found Sherri Moon's Lily to be appealing and likeable. She dives headlong into it and I think it's one of her most successful parts. Don't @ me.

So yeah, overall, I had fun. I don't think it's a movie you can judge by putting it up against a 90s Addams Family flick or even the *Casper* remake, because it's not those. And really, it isn't meant to be, not in Rob Zombie's monster mind. We have enough of those anyway, don't we?

This is a movie that's meant to celebrate a wonderful fictional world in which Cassandra Peterson plays someone who isn't Elvira, where old Universal Monster movies appear on new book and album covers, and where a newly resurrected creature stitched together from different bodies can start a psychobilly comedy horror punk band and gain instant fame.

I love all of that.

Just A Little Creepy by PRIMM

Walking through the graveyard

When you feel a gentle breeze

Everything goes silent

Except the rustling of the leaves

A sudden flash of movement

Where'd it go? Where is it at?

It pounces out in front of you

It's just an alley cat

You're headed to the basement

And you make this trip at night

A couple sharp quick twinkles

and *Poof!* out goes the light

You hear a shift and then a slide

You holler out, "Who's there?"

A box falls on the floor before you

SHOOOM! You're up the stairs

You're sitting home alone at night

A storm with driving rain

All at once you hear it

A tapping on the pane

A sudden flash of lightning

You decide to take a chance

Investigate the window

Take a look...It's just a branch

So many simple little things

To keep us on our toes

It's just a little creepy

Then again, who really knows?

THE FLINT HORROR COLLECTIVE PRESENTS:

MIDNIGHT MUSEUM
Horror Marketplace

OCTOBER 29, 2022, 12 - 5 PM

Horror artists, authors, crafters, vendors

Interactive surprises

FREE

PLUS

LORDS OF OCTOBER ANNUAL HALLOWEEN PARTY
From 6-10 PM Join Lords for their CD RELEASE, "CRYPTOZOOLOGY"
With Special Guests:
STIFLING EDITH and BLACK SWAN DIVE BOMB
Plus costume contests and other tricks and treats!
ALL AGES - FLINT LOCAL 432

USS EDSON
Hauntings on the River

Aside from numerous deployments over several decades for use in different areas, the USS Edson, a Forrest-Sherman Class destroyer of the United States Navy, has a seriously strange distinction. Aside from the legends of hauntings that have been suggested after numerous eyewitness accounts, the Edson has the historical privilege of being used in an episode of the classic horror/sci-fi television

show The Twilight Zone. The episode in question is called "The Thirty Fathom Grave" and features the crew of a Navy destroyer bearing their own scary witness to a series of spooky sounds coming from a long sunken submarine.

Some might consider that information to be an initial source of the purported eventual haunting, with misinformation and suggestibility bringing a myth to life. But it could also be just a bizarre, coincidental precursor to the odd haunted ship stories reported by multiple people after visits to the old vessel, now repurposed as the Saginaw Valley Naval Ship Museum.

But before getting too far into the alleged ghostly aspects of said museum, perhaps some history is necessary for context. The Edson, named after General Merritt Edson, a Medal of Honor and Navy Cross winning commanding officer in World War 2, having served more than 30 years in active duty to his country. When "Red Mike" (Merritt's nickname) passed away in 1955, his widow sponsored the laying down of the ship, a ceremony that the shipbuilding company

Bath Iron Works Corporation attended, and construction on the destroyer got underway.

After its formal commission in 1958, the Edson was used for the next few decades for a variety of Naval campaigns, including patrol, search, and rescue duties in ports and mainland as far reaching as Taiwan, The Philippines, and Vietnam, the latter of which earned the ship the moniker "The Grey Ghost of the Vietnamese Coast". Over that time period and other stages of operation, the Edson was hit by North Vietnamese coastal artillery, friendly fire from the U.S. Air Force, and had a fire start in the fireroom before being decommissioned as the last remaining all-gun destroyer in the Navy.

In 2004, the Saginaw Valley Naval Ship Museum put forth the proposal to allow the destroyer to be moved and used as a museum, and in 2012 it was finally approved to make the trip along the Saginaw River to be anchored for museum use.

In the time since the Edson became a permanent fixture at her permanent site, strange happenings have been reported by both museum workers and visitors alike. The president of the museum himself has alleged that tools relocate from place to place, and on occasion his own car has started by itself if it was parked near the ship. This is sometimes thought of in paranormal circles as a "phantom vehicle", and as odd as it sounds, there are asserted precedents in the form of vehicular hauntings in which a car turns on or sometimes even moves by itself.

In Germany, a 1945 Volkswagen Beetle is said to have started up and rammed into a wall without a driver. Most famously perhaps, in South Africa, witnesses reported a car that was "jumping" even though the engine was off, and as recently as 2018, in Singapore, there was a dash-cam recording that reportedly showed a "ghost car" that was the cause of a multi-car crash. Some researchers have asserted that the paranormal energy surrounding a location could possibly be the source of such a rare activity.

Since the Edson is open for tours, customers have noticed other unusual occurrences as varied as footsteps emanating from an empty area and whispers that seem to come from out of nowhere. Some investigators, such as the crew from the TV show Ghost Asylum, assert that the sounds and other events could be due to the double hauntings of a suicidal officer and a phantom watchman. Ghost Asylum's ghost hunters even uncovered what they felt was evidence of the battleship being haunted, with their paranormal equipment and EMF (Electromagnetic Field Meter) readers going off the charts with active readings that may have signified the presence and even attempted communication from trapped spirits.

Carla Monteiro, the Edson's communication director, has publicly acknowledged the assertions of the phantom watchman, noting that a psychic once made contact with the wayward security guard, claiming that he was friendly and that his name is Paul. This same psychic also offered that Paul was the one who was playfully making himself known by starting the president's car and rolling down the windows. She also claims to have actually seen him.

Carla said the outline of a man walked past her on a personal tour of the Edson, and that a feeling like "static electricity" came over her when he appeared. She has also offered that different guests have reported the appearance of a ghost dog on the decks below, perhaps the ghostly pet of the lonely night watchman?

Aside from the ghost hunting tours, the Edson is now the site of a seasonal haunted attraction, an onboard haunt called The Edson Incident. The Edson employees take advantage of the revered battleship/museum's spooky natural setting and rumored hauntings to scare people every Halloween, and a visitor to the attraction might indeed wonder if there are other eyes watching from the hallowed, storied deck of the "Grey Ghost of Bay City".

HALLOWEEN JOKES BY MARK TAYLOR

Why don't mummies take time off? They're afraid to unwind!

Why did the vampire read the newspaper? He heard it had great circulation.

What's a pumpkin's favorite genre?  Pulp fiction.

Where do ghosts buy their food? At the ghost-ery store!

HALLOWEEN STORE SIGHTINGS

WHERE DO WE START?!

As we said earlier in this issue, Halloween 2022 has brought a TON of cool Halloween tricks and treats from a multitude of places. Over the past few years, Target has really stepped up with their Halloween décor and overall offerings, so much so that it seems to have affected the output of even rival Walmart. So, let's take a deep look at Target with our Halloween pals!

Isaiah and Audri (can you find her in the pic? are both REALLY fond of this banjo playing Halloween skeleton. It really is an entertaining animatronic and sets the tone for Target's 2022 output.

Those super cool gargoyle statues are also striking and would look amazing in pretty much any home haunt or Halloween party.

The aisles at our Target (Flint Township, Michigan) were just full to the brim with awesome Halloween stuff. Entire sections for Halloween foodies, costumes, décor.

Anakin ADORES this light up bat powered tombstone. This would look amazing at night or in a dark display.

Meanwhile, Miley got a big kick out of this creepy, otherworldy telephone.

She probably had a (one-sided) back and forth conversation for a good 5 minutes.

Aubri carried this All Hallow's pal around with her pretty much through the entire store.

16 | HALLOWEEN MACHINE AUTUMN 2022

Let's talk about the enchanting box art on this year's batch of Halloween cereals!! Though it's a bit disappointing that these weren't new flavors, the art is so great, and the milk changes to Halloween colors, so that's always gonna be fun.

All these traditional cereals got new box art too, with little changes like spooky marshmallows. The big exception here is the brand new Hocus Pocus 2 cereal, which, along with super appealing Halloween art, offered a new flavor of cereal.

Sometimes these seasonal type cereals don't taste like anything very unique or don't tend to stand out much, but Hocus Pocus 2 cereal has a pretty good flavor. Almost reminds me of my beloved Smurf Berry Crunch from years ago.

So yeah, Hocus Pocus 2 for the win!

SPIRIT HALLOWEEN

This year, our buddy Audri got hired at Spirit Halloween! As you can imagine, this was a very exciting development for all of us, and Audri even scored the brand new Regan animatronic early on! Here's a quick look at some of Spirit's great stuff this season.

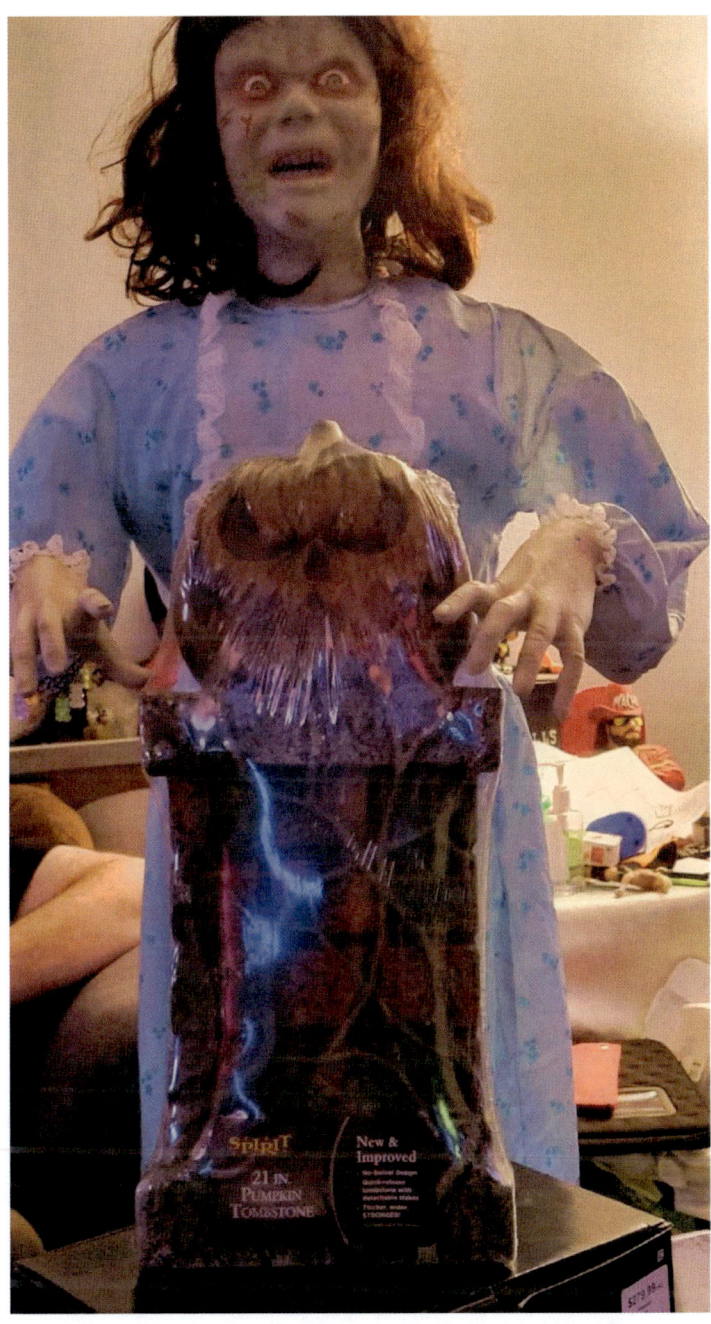

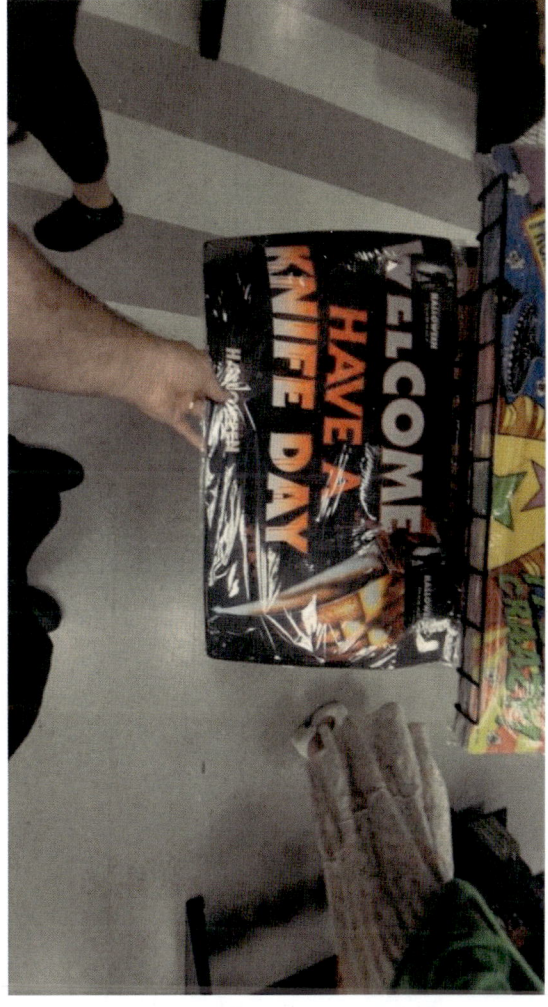

MICHAELS

Michaels is pretty much always loaded with spooky cool and unique stuff, and this year is no different. Audri and big sis Makayla show us some of their fave stuff from Michaels 2022 collection.

KROGER, SAMS, CHRISTMAS TREES…AND THAT

The Monster Mash: Halloween's #1 Song for 60 Years...And Running

(Revised from its original publication on RueMorgue.com)

By Paul Counelis

It might seem strange to dedicate an entire article to what is fairly easily the most popular genre related song ever made. Horror fans the world over are WELL aware of the significant impact of "Monster Mash". But October 2022 marks the 60th Halloween that this song has reigned supreme for the playlists of America's favorite dark holiday, and it is still converting kids to the fantastic world of monsters; when my daughter Miley was only 3, her favorite book was a pop-out Hallmark type that plays the song when you push the colorful buttons along the side.

It also doesn't hurt that I have a decent sized collection of all things "Monster Mash" related, including umpteen different variations of a singing, dancing Frankie. Simply put, I adore this tune and have argued for and will continue to argue about its status as one of the greatest songs ever written; after all, what song is more truly immortal than one that's routinely played over and over at parties every single year without fail?

BTW, don't answer that with "Happy Birthday to You".

Still, there's another reason…in 2007 I was writing for a (now defunct) publication and was given the green light to delve into Bobby Pickett's wonderful ditty, as well as get an update on what Bobby was up to. I wrote to the e-mail address on his official page, requesting an online interview. The response was a bit cryptic, in retrospect: "Bobby prefers phone interviews. Good luck." Included was Pickett's home phone number. I was ecstatic.

I had a bunch of different deadlines to get to, and the "Monster Mash" piece was pushed back by the editor, so a couple of months went by. One morning only a few days after I had prepared the interview questions, I woke up to the shocking news of Bobby Pickett's passing. I hadn't been aware of his recent illness and was floored and saddened to read the details on his website.

Ever since, I've felt kind of like I owed him one. After all, for all of the song's popularity and its beloved status in the horror community (and beyond), there really aren't a lot of features exploring the origins and history of "Monster Mash" and Pickett's other creative ventures.

But the biggest reason is that of all the songs, images and icons of the modern era, maybe no single piece of work is more easily identified with the mainstream horror genre as the 1962 hit. You hear it every year at Halloween parties, in movie and TV soundtracks, commercials, and it's even represented by toys and other memorabilia.

Bobby Pickett was a horror movie fan and nightclub performer when he co-wrote this amazingly popular monster anthem with band member Leonard Capizzi in May of 1962. Pickett had been performing a rendition of The Diamonds' hit "Little Darling" using an impression of horror master Boris Karloff, which audiences loved. Capizzi encouraged Bobby to write a song based on the Karloff vocals, and "Monster Mash" was the result of their collaboration.

The song was a play on popular dance songs of the era, smash hits like "Mashed Potato" and Chubby Checker's "The Twist", the latter of which had reached #1 on the American charts only two years before in 1960. With Bobby's uncanny

impression of Uncle Boris to fuel the single, as well as a brief but also excellent imitation of Bela Lugosi's legendary voice ("Whatever happened to my Transylvania Twist?"), it was originally passed on by literally every major record label.

Legendary novelty producer Gary S. Paxton heard the song and decided to engineer and produce it. Paxton

also played on the song, credited as a member of "The Cryptkickers", along with Leon Russell, Johnny McCrae, Terry Berg, and Rickie Page. The song was released as a single and became a HUGE smash just before Halloween of 1962, going all the way to number one on the charts, where it remained for two weeks.

"Monster Mash" is a curious song in the annals of music history for more than one reason. First, the song was actually banned by the BBC in 1962, cited as being "too morbid" for mainstream airplay. Also, the song was re-released as a single and actually re-entered the American charts in 1962, 1970, and 1973, a very rare accomplishment, and one that helped to cement the status of the legendary monster single. Here's how rare it actually is: it's the ONLY song ever to reach the top 100 on three separate occasions, a feat that Pickett was extremely proud of.

Happily, it was finally released in the UK in 1973 (in October, naturally) and this time went to #3 on the UK charts. In another astounding development, the song actually re-entered the UK charts 25 years later in 2008, peaking at #60.

Pickett, who at one point before the song's recording was an aspiring actor, welcomed the massive success of his monstrous hit but was never again able to duplicate it with any new singles. He did enjoy modest success with a Christmas tinged "sequel" of sorts, late 1962's "Monster's Holiday" which charted at #30. He entered the charts again in 1963 with the song "Graduation Day", peaking at #80 and then dropping off of the charts almost immediately.

"Monster Mash" gained popularity over the succeeding years, so much so that it inspired and spawned other original songs, cover versions (the seminal punk group The Misfits' recording is especially beloved), even books and films. Of course, the song has never lost its relevancy during that most ghoulish holiday celebration, Halloween. For monster film fans, the song can be heard on multiple films and TV shows, including the

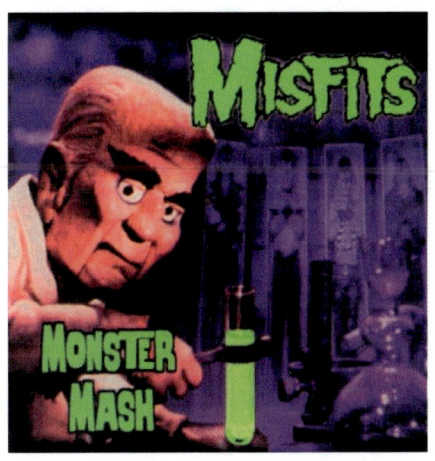

polarizing film sequel *Halloween III: Season of the Witch*. Every year the song is heard all throughout the month of October and is an enduring tribute to its ambitious singer and co-writer and his love of the horror genre.

Boris Karloff himself is said to have adored the recording, so much so that he actually "sang" a version of the song during a 1965 broadcast of the show "Shindig!" There's a wonderful clip from the show floating around the internet of Karloff speak/singing the lyrics of the first verse and chorus.

Known as the "Guy Lombardo of Halloween", Pickett remained prolific with his performing in the years to follow, becoming a fan favorite on Barry Hansen's "Dr. Demento" radio show. He continued to perform "Monster Mash" and his other horrific hits at different venues throughout the world, even appearing live at the televised third "Horror Hall of Fame Awards" hosted by horror great (and the original Freddy Krueger) Robert Englund where he sang "Monster Mash" to a delighted crowd of horror fans.

Pickett co-wrote a musical with author Sheldon Allman in 1967 with one of the greatest titles of all time, *I'm Sorry the Bridge is Out, You'll Have to Spend the Night*, and another a few years later called *Frankenstein Unbound*. The latter was developed by the co-writers of Disney/Pixar's *Toy Story* as a film called *Frankenstein Sings*. The title was changed again to *Monster Mash: The Movie* to reflect the enduring popularity of Pickett's now legendary single. Pickett himself appeared in the film, along with Candace Cameron of "Full House" fame. Incidentally, it's one of my daughter Audri's very favorite flicks.

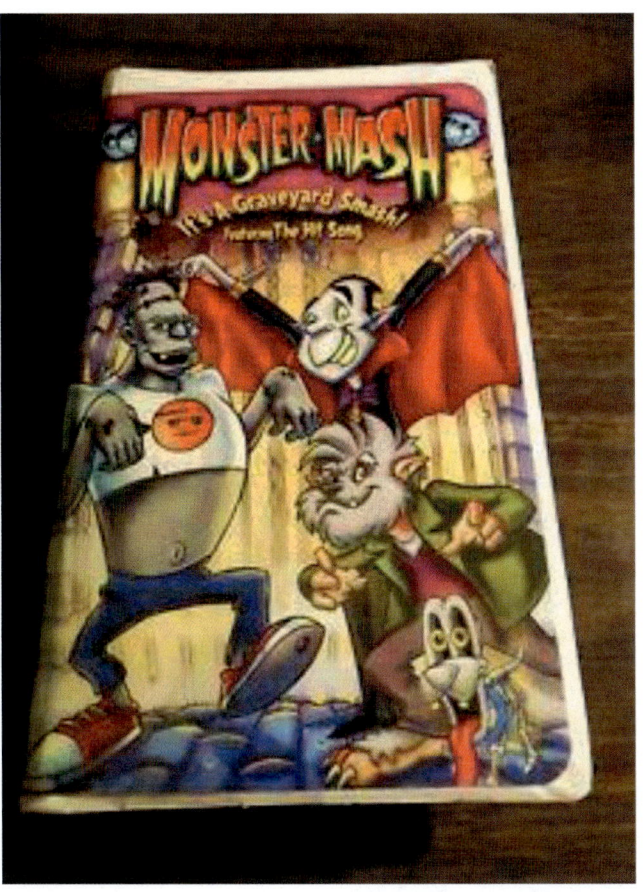

Pickett wrote and released his autobiography in 2005: *Monster Mash: Half Dead in Hollywood* can be purchased at Pickett's official website, themonstermash.com, along with other works and Monster Mash related memorabilia.

Sadly, Pickett passed away in April of 2007. His legacy, however, is in absolutely no danger of becoming irrelevant, as generation after generation will be doing the Monster Mash for years and years to come. The song's overwhelming universality is a lasting and immortal tribute to its creator, Bobby "Boris" Pickett. It's a legacy that will be celebrated by the gathering ghouls every Halloween season at party after party, with the inevitability that yes, the scene will be rocking, and all will be digging the sound.

THE HANSON HOUSE
BY KIDDFERD P

I always thought the house on the corner of our street seemed a little, you know, iffy. Like not the house itself, but what was LEFT of it. People talked about tearing it down, but nobody ever approached it to take action. So it sat there, like a giant eye watching us and waiting. For what? I kinda hope we never find out.

My friends Destiny, Oliver, Jackson, Haven, and I planned on braving AT LEAST the porch this Halloween.

Legend has it that kids that make it to the porch get treasures untold, because they have to promise not to tell what they get. Some say it's a giant candy bar, others say it's all the pop you can carry. Whatever it is, only three kids ever succeeded, and they ran off smiling and never spoke of it. Who does that?!?

Now, how they can find treasures in an old abandoned dilapidated house is beyond me, but my 13 year old mind HAD to see for myself. I had to know what it was that was up there, and what the reward was.

When I told the clan what I wanted to do, Destiny started quoting from her Dad's medical journals about the heart and how it can only take SO much before it gives out and stops. She's always afraid of some crazy medical thing happening that nobody has ever heard of and doesn't even really want to know is possible. Anyways, Oliver said "I think we should at least consider that there could actually be a treasure up there. Nobody has been up there for years, and if you sit in the study at My Mom's desk, you can hear noises coming from the house all the time. Something is definitely in the house... I say we go and check it out."

Haven hit her brother hard and said "I've heard the noises too, and if we're gonna go in there, we're gonna need to take protection." That's where Jackson comes in. He's Destiny's older brother- the dreamy one, with eyes like a summer sky. He sees things that nobody else sees, and stuff just happens when he's around, like fear doesn't exist and magic steps in and takes over. I love Jackson. He's gonna be my boyfriend one day. So Destiny and I set out to recruit him for our Halloween plan.

We started out with things like "Doesn't this sound like fun?!" And "I like your hair." (That was me.) At first he didn't want to be a part of it, but he eventually agreed when we offered him $5 each, and Destiny promised she would stay on the sidewalk.

I went home and set out my costume for the next day... THE day... Halloween day!

I woke up the next morning scared and excited. Grabbed my Wonder Woman costume, complete with the cape, boots, armbands, invisible lasso and head band, and ran off to find some of my mom's lipstick. We all decided to meet after school in Oliver's yard, since he lived right next door to the corner house. Haven and I grabbed hands, and followed closely behind Jackson, who was leading the way. Oliver stayed back with Destiny, Probably to make sure she wasn't too afraid.

The three of us crept up the old broken steps and stopped sharp. There in the corner lay an old gray dog, the size of a wolf. He didn't move much, just let his eyes follow our movements and closed 'em back up when we stopped walking. Jackson caught his breath then, like he was winded, and Haven shrieked and made a run for home. Jackson closed his eyes and started to hum. The humming sounded familiar to me, and right away I felt a sense of deja vu, like this had all happened before.

I slipped my hand into Jackson's hand, and held on as hard as I could. Jackson opened his eyes and without acknowledging the wolf-dog headed straight for the door. He swung the bulky, dusty door open and we walked forward slowly, not sure what we were expecting to see. Jackson headed straight to the mantle and picked up a muddy covered glass picture frame that looked older than the house. It was a picture of a girl with dark curly hair, and the cutest smile.

She was wearing a long dress, but the frame had broken and the picture had started to fade, so we couldn't see the bottom of it. I wondered what her shoes looked like then, if she was the kind of girl who wore boots, or cute strappy shoes. I forgot to be afraid. We were about to turn away from the mantle when I felt the stare... I swung around so quickly that Jackson startled and dropped the picture. When it hit the ground, the frame smashed into tiny bits and the picture was clear. I was staring straight into my own eyes, and started screaming. Jackson swung around and said softly, "Marlane, you ok?"

I told him what I saw and he said that he saw it too. He then told me there was someone behind us, and I should close my eyes and not look. I tried to listen to him, I REALLY did, but I just HAD to know who or what was behind me. I twirled around and was almost face to face with the wolf-dog. He was standing on his hind legs and was taller than me, but I didn't feel afraid.

As sudden as he was behind me, he was back out on the porch sleeping. The frame was back in Jackson's hand, and he was saying something about how the girl looked like me. I started to laugh when I realized what was happening. The house was literally rewinding us again, and pushing us out, just like it had every Halloween for the past few years. The kids that made it in were US... me, Jackson, and Oliver. Destiny always waited on the sidewalk.

We had taken photographs each year and dropped them on the floor to prove that we had been there before, but every picture had been cleaned up, and the feeling of deja vu was actually a memory in reverse. I started laughing louder now, which made Jackson laugh, and we backed out onto the porch, smiling. Jackson turned to me and said, "Each year I show you a little more, and every year you remember a little less." Then he grabbed my hand and led me home, both of us still smiling and knowing we would be back the next year, to see what we could discover on Halloween night at the Hanson House.

TEN Family Frightfests

10 MOVIES TO WATCH WITH YOUR FAMILY FOR HALLOWEEN
by Paul Counelis

10. The Monster Squad (1987, PG-13) – Fred Dekker's comedic clash of the classic monsters is a perfect bridge from the more mild, "Scooby-Doo" type prepubescent material to a bit more sophistication – but only a bit. The fun stuff stays. The Monster Squad is entertaining from start to finish, featuring appropriate updates of the Universal Monsters, a great cast of kids, memorable lines, and Michael Sembello's relentlessly catchy ode to eighties synth cheese "Rock Until You Drop". You'll be slapping your head for weeks trying to get that little ditty out of your mind.

9. The Gate (1987, PG-13) – The Gate is the other great family horror film from 1987, but with somewhat less comedy and a more heightened sense of spooky. A group of kids accidentally unleash demons from a hole in the backyard, and now they gotta save the world. Stephen Dorff made his theatrical debut with this little gem, remembered by many children of the nineties as the first time they saw (and subsequently loved) a scary movie.

8. The Witches (1990, PG) – Child literature visionary Roald Dahl (Charlie and the Chocolate Factory) penned The Witches, an atmospheric, creepy look at a group of witches who want to rid the world of children. The catch is that the one person who knows about the plan is a young orphan boy that the witches have turned into a mouse. It's somewhat dark and very entertaining, with a memorable turn by Anjelica Huston as the Grand High Witch.

7. Dark Night of the Scarecrow (1981, Made for TV) – Widely considered by many horror fans to be one of the best TV movies ever made since its release during Halloween of '81, Dark Night of the Scarecrow is both a scary visual treat and an engrossing story full of pathos. A mentally ill man named Bubba is erroneously hunted down by a group of angry townspeople after a tragedy involving a little girl. In the most effective climactic scenes, a scarecrow stalks Bubba's attackers one by one, the apparent victims of a paranormal vigilante. It is a thoughtful and creepy movie for younger and older viewers alike. "Bubba didn't do it!"

6. Twilight Zone: The Movie (1983, PG) – Classic stories from the TV series are revisited by four big-time directors with somewhat mixed results, but the overall package of Twilight Zone: The Movie is entertaining and eerie, with arguably the

most memorable moment occurring during the John Landis directed prologue. "You wanna see something REALLY scary?"

5. ParaNorman (2012, PG) – ParaNorman returned only modest box office receipts despite its big marketing push, but it is the perfect family frightfest, full of zombies, witches and ghosts. Combining stunning 3D stop-motion animation with humor, some pretty unique scary moments and a heaping of heart, ParaNorman exhibits a lyrical poetry with just the right amount of spooky that should appeal to adults and children alike.

4. Lady in White (1988, PG-13) – A throwback ghost story/mystery genre mash-up with high interest to fans of haunted house stories, Lady in White boasts a great Halloween feel and atmosphere. It's scary, but not TOO scary, and another movie that leaves viewers humming an incessantly catchy song.

3. The Bad Seed (1956) – The Bad Seed still holds quite a high measure of tension with the story of an evil little girl played by Patty McCormack, who received a rare horror related Academy Award nomination for her performance. The movie is dark and edgy, and the climax of the film will likely leave a strong impression on young viewers. Features one of the strangest credit roll sequences in cinematic history; must be seen to be believed.

2. Watership Down (1978, PG) – One of the most unusual animated features ever produced, Watership Down features some challenging subject matter that attempts to stay true to the nature of the original novel about a group of rabbits forced to flee their home and search for a new one. There are plenty of jolts and some inevitable tugging of the heartstrings. It was feared that the theatrical poster for the movie would be too off-putting for children, despite the even more dark content of the film itself.

1. The Birds (1963, PG-13) – The master of suspense Alfred Hitchcock concocted this nail-bitingly scary story about birds rising up to viciously attack the people of a town in California. The Birds is a tense, well-crafted thriller that leaves audiences of any age unable to veer attention away from the screen. The film illustrates the notion of the right storyteller being able to make even the most docile of creatures seem terrifying.

For those who haven't heard, Apple TV has a series called "The Snoopy Show" that is made up of new cartoons featuring our favorite Peanuts characters in new stories. This is obviously great news to those of us who are so fond of the legendary *It's the Great Pumpkin, Charlie Brown*, especially when we discover that the Peanuts are celebrating Halloween again!

Season 1 Episode 3 is such a charming take on Halloween, at that. It is comprised of several different "shorts", and they are all kind of warm and fun. The episode is titled "The Curse of a Funny Face", and the standout one here shows Snoopy doing all sorts of elaborate "tricks" instead of just giving out treats.

35 | HALLOWEEN MACHINE   AUTUMN 2022

They are all loaded with iconic Halloween imagery and gorgeous, vibrant, seasonal colors. Even the most jaded among us should manage to get that warm Halloween feeling from these cartoons. The other episodes include Snoopy watching a scary movie and Snoopy helping Charlie Brown find a suitable costume.

While the writing is clearly not Charles M. Schulz, the characters are sufficiently in keeping with how we have grown to expect them to react. Snoopy is as clever and funny as ever, for instance. Check this one out if you get a chance. Great Halloweeny fun for the whole family. We might never get a sequel to *Great Pumpkin*, but this is a pretty fun addition to the yearly All Hallow's watch list.

37 | HALLOWEEN MACHINE   AUTUMN 2022

Macabre Music THE DOORS

By Paul Counelis

This time around instead of taking one specific record and calling it a "horror" album, I wanted to take an overall look at the band that has my vote for one of the most truly spiritually strange catalogs in rock history: The Doors.

This is largely due, of course, to the presence of rock's sacred midnight angel, Jim Morrison. He is the most obvious reason that The Doors retain their air of mystique 50 years on, appealing to generation after generation with the unique blend of Morrison's weirdest poetic incantations and the band's dangerous brand of scary bluesman jazz rock. In short, their frontman had something that most of even the most outwardly creepy death rock and horror punk creators don't…a true heart of darkness.

For every lyric telling of the beauty of a woman or "the way she walks" Morrison penned two devilishly supernatural odes, and even the brightest Doors songs (think "Light My Fire", "I Looked at You") had "wolves" in them. In the form of Morrison's voice, yes, but also that eerie Vox Continental combo organ that the underrated Ray Manzarek seemed to pull hellish melodies from and guitarist Robby Krieger's ghostly Gibson noodlings.

A song like "Moonlight Drive" can barely be contained by its own recording, Krieger and Manzarek teaming up with the offbeat, accenting John Densmore on drums and putting you directly into a dark, moonlit night, fog over the ocean, Morrison's pleads of moon swimming fading into morbidly alluring refrains of drowning together.

That's Morrison's idea of romance…swimming to the moon, disappearing through the tide, penetrating the night itself, never to be seen again. And of course, in context this comes on the "heels" of the ghastly poetry of "Horse Latitudes", which tells the quick, creepy tale of a still sea whose currents breed tiny monsters that "jettison" the animals of the title in "mute nostril agony".

Simply put, in the late sixties, The Doors were the nightmare answer to the flower generation, with Morrison's charismatic delivery keeping them in mass popularity despite the Beatles' unparalleled reign and stuff like The Monkees' "Daydream Believer" owning the airwaves.

Go ahead and cheer up, Sleepy Jean…but when the music's over, turn out the lights.

From their first record, the self-titled THE DOORS (which remains one of the greatest and most startling debut albums in rock history, right there with BLACK SABBATH and VAN HALEN), clearly The Doors had a different agenda than dancing hippies into the seventies. The sullen, brooding poem in E Minor echoed a Celine novel and included lines direct from a William Blake poem (one of the extremely well read Morrison's heroes) was issued as a B-side to the more subtly black "Break On Through (To the

Other Side)" and is still effective to this day.

EVERY Doors record contains alchemy; legitimate creep factor stuff like "Texas Radio and the Big Beat" coming out of the swamp, of course the highway nightmare "Riders on the Storm" (which Morrison literally envisioned as a horror film), the Dionysian hellfire of "The End", the quiet, building darkness of "When the Music's Over" (complete with Morrison's plea to hear 'the scream of the butterfly'), the call and response acapella "My Wild Love" in which the singer's love rides to the Devil and asks him to 'pay'…and on and on and on. Strange days have found us…strange days have tracked us down.

The Doors were not a "horror" band, but they were most definitely a band of horrors, greeting the darkness head on and with the spirit of which one would embrace an old friend. For all the howling and growling of many of the blackest metal groups, you'd be hard pressed to believe that someone was in closer contact with the darkest powers-that-be than James Douglas Morrison.

And this is only a small sample of the horrors contained in those scant few studio records; there are several symphonies of the 'bright midnight' on every single Doors album; dripping with the ghosts of Morrison's mind, echoing through the creative renderings of the remaining Doors' dances with the Devil himself.

As a band, I give The Doors 5 out of 5 pumpkins, if I'm allowed to do so, and while it's true that some are born to sweet delight, Morrison is an alchemic reminder in human form that some are born to the endless night.

THE HALLOWEEN THAT ALMOST WASN'T

Every year around the middle of August or so, when the craft stores and candle makers are putting out their early Halloween goodies despite the dissenting cries of whiny Christmas lovin' "Tweeters" everywhere, that autumn whisper sends its first chilly hint of what's to come. It's there in the earlier nights and the subtle hue change of the ever green leaves; just a small breath whispered on the late summer wind…*I'm coming*.

At my house, that means dreaming of those fall nights spent outside listening to scary movie themes and readying our October displays for that perfect spooky mood. Inevitably, we wind up eating candied and caramel apples and watching horror oriented shows, and depending on how early the youngest child falls asleep, we have to find some family programming that won't scare the little one TOO much, but won't be a chore for the rest of us to sit through.

The most fun Halloween movies and episodes are the ones that are easily re-visited for their ease at delivering the Halloween spirit. *The Halloween That Almost Wasn't* isn't the most challenging or hardcore horror telefilm, but there's a definite nostalgia that will probably be present for children of the seventies and eighties, even if you haven't seen it before.

The Halloween That Almost Wasn't, inexplicably renamed *The Night Dracula*

Saved the World for VHS release, was originally intended to become one of those annual specials that surface every year during holiday seasons, much like the heavyweight *The Grinch Who Stole Christmas* or any number of Rankin-Bass specials we see every winter. As such, it's honestly not in the same realm quality wise.

But horror and Halloween fans are more apt to like something just because it's strange and unique; we tend to find a beauty (as it were) in things that many people would completely sneer at. That's not to say that *The Halloween That Almost Wasn't* doesn't have its own virtues and appeal; as a spooky entry level charmer, it's perfect for a horror fan to watch with a small child.

The movie was released in October of 1979, and there is an undeniable seventies influence throughout, from the casting of the actors (*Taxi*'s Judd Hirsch as Dracula?) to the nods to the commercially prevalent music of the era, disco. Depending on your point of view, those influences could be charming or grating. For a child, it won't matter either way, and they'll likely just enjoy seeing all the monsters summoned to Dracula's castle for a huge monster pow wow.

The plot is simple; in a nutshell, on a Transylvanian newscast Dracula is blamed for what might be the demise of Halloween. In turn, he points the fingers at ALL the monsters, who have gotten so complacent with their status as monsters (EX: the Wolfman has been doing ads for razors) that they have ceased to be scary. So Drac invites the whole lot of them (Frankenstein's Monster, a zombie, Wolfman, Mummy, a witch) to his spooky crib with the goal being to make them scary again so Halloween can continue on it's dark, happy path.

The witch (Mariette Hartley…more odd casting) is the one who started the rumor of Halloween's demise, mostly because she doesn't feel like celebrating the holiday anymore. For some unexplainable reason, Halloween cannot continue unless the witch flies over the moon. A group of trick or treaters restore her Halloween spirit and confidence, and the only thing left is for Drac to live up to a ridiculous (and charmingly dated---again, depending on your POV) promise he made to her: disco dance in his Transylvanian home.

The Emmy winning short telefilm was directed by Bruce Bilson, a longtime television veteran. Character actor John Schuck, one of those "Hey, I've seen that guy in other stuff" types, played the very Herman Munster-y Frankenstein Monster in *The Halloween That Almost Wasn't*, and reunited with Bilson a few years later to portray Herman in the somewhat less charmingly dated *The Munsters Today*.

Like a lot of other forgotten mini-gems from that era, *The Halloween That Almost Wasn't* has never gotten a DVD release. It's not too hard to track down a VHS copy if you want to check it out for yourself. At the very least, it's a Halloweenish, pleasant intro for younger children into our favorite genre and an odd, smile inducing jaunt for a more seasoned horror fan.

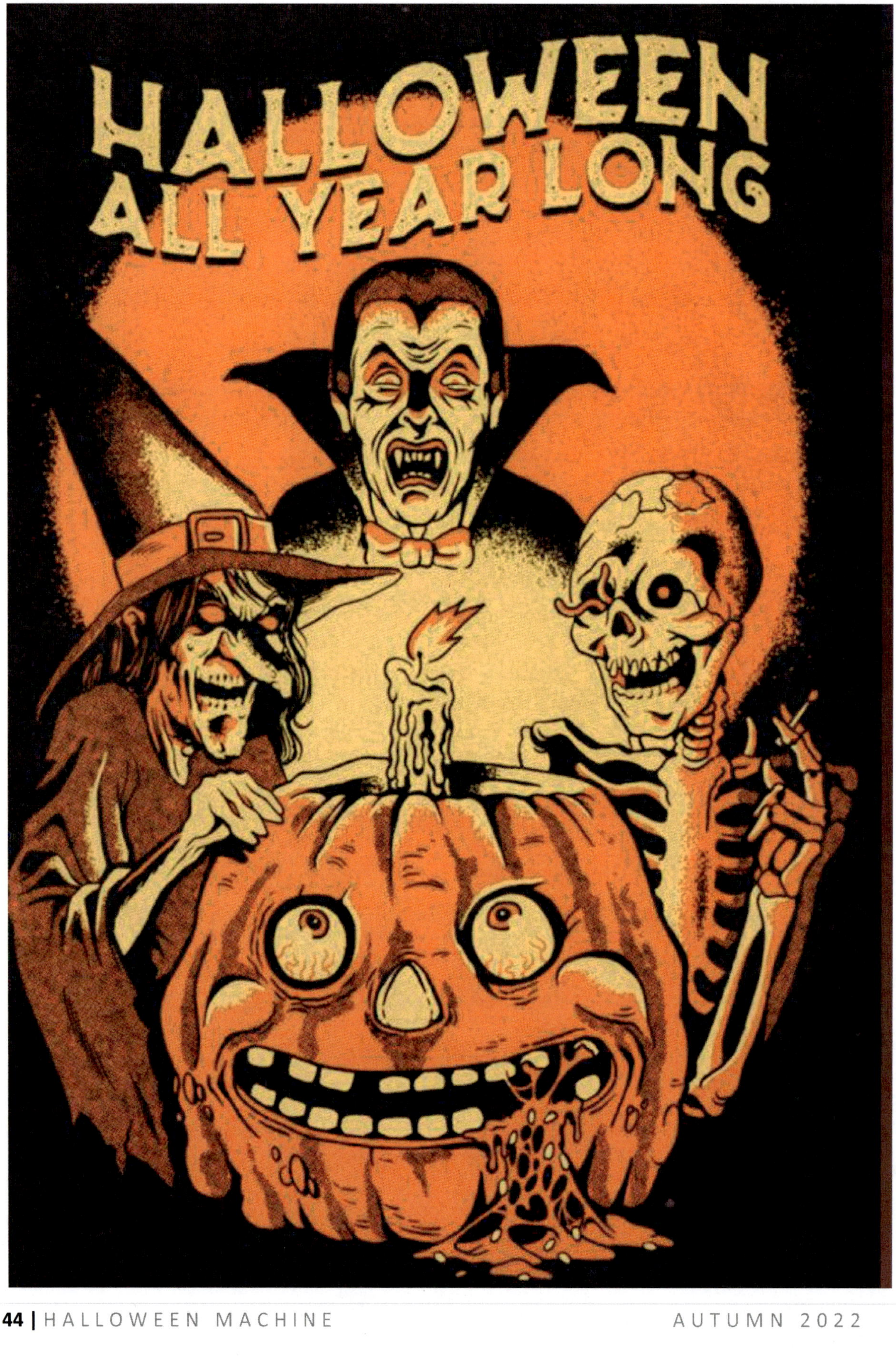
HALLOWEEN
ALL YEAR LONG

Open Graves
Kurtis Primm

Through the mists one Halloween
There came a sight I've never seen
A group of bones out having fun
A roving band of skeletons

No costumes here, for they were real
Cavorting for some fun to steal
I watched them go from door to door
A sight I'd never seen before

Each one with a sack in hand
This jingling, jangling boney band
They roamed the Jack O' Lantern streets
And filled their sacks with trick or treats

And with the ending of the night
They shambled off just out of sight
I rushed to see just where they'd go
The cemetery up the road

And with the hour getting late
They filed through the iron gate
They offered up a parting wave
Then slunk back in their open graves

Those Magical Halloween Nights!

I can pinpoint one of the main magical nights that fed my Halloween obsession:

Hanging out with the Randols on the Eastside of Flint, Michigan.

We went out Trick or Treating early evening. The night was perfect, just like in the movies...overcast sky, not too cold. In retrospect, I was probably "too old" to Trick or Treat by many peoples' standards, but really just a big enthusiastic kid, so it evened out. ☺

We decided to RUN to every house, and did so for a few blocks straight without stopping.

After cleaning up the immediate neighborhood in like half an hour, with the sky clearing and under a now visible moon, we decided to venture further out and headed to a "richer" neighborhood.

As soon as we made it across the street, we could hear laughter and see a bunch of very well decorated houses.

There was a bit of natural striking imagery, with the light of the moon framing a huge pile of orange and rosy-hued leaves in front of a fence separating the streets. So memorable that we all stopped and commented on how cool it looked.

We headed further into the night, hitting every street for a few blocks, then started the trek home. On the way back through, a few houses emptied their candy bowls into our pillow cases, then shut their porch lights off behind us.

We made it back to "our" neighborhood, virtually the only people still wandering the evening aside from a few stray cars here and there. It was very quiet, and the smell of the night was unmistakably autumn.

We stopped at the little store a couple blocks from the house to get a drink, which the super friendly store clerk gave us for free. We had been gone for literally hours, and our full candy bags reflected our efforts. We talked excitedly about the Halloween haul and made plans to do even more the next year.

That night around 1 AM, I was the only one awake. I was watching scary movies very quietly in the living room, and for some reason while getting a drink, I decided to step outside onto the porch.

The night was now enveloped by the most autumnal presence, both sight and smell. The stillness was remarkable. I closed my eyes and took a deep breath, savoring the magic.

Today, when we spend literal hundreds of dollars every Halloween to build our haunt and add to its existing elements, every penny seems worth it. The efforts of so many people go into it, from the building to the decorating, from the hours of acting on Halloween night to the clean-up in the days that follow.

We keep coming back to it, and I am so glad we do...because I carry that special Halloween night with me, and rain or shine, I know that we're helping to contribute to a magical night for so many Trick or Treaters...maybe even the kind of experience that they'll look back on in twenty years with a fond recollection and the thought, "I can pinpoint my love for Halloween to this one magical night..."

ART BY DIAMOND COUNELIS

HAPPY HALLOWEEN FROM HALLOWEEN MACHINE

If you have anything you'd like to share in these hallowed pages, please drop us a line at HalloweenMachineMagazine1@gmail.com and show us what ya got!